What activity do you do for fun?

CURIO
Questions & answers about...
Rainforests

What's your favourite rainforest animal?

Have you ever been in a forest?

Do you prefer rainy or sunny weather?

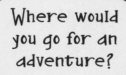

Where would you go for an adventure?

Would you like to live in the treetops or on the forest floor?

Words by Anne Rooney

Illustrations by Mike Moran

MILES KELLY

What is a rainforest?

It's a MASSIVE crowd of trees and animals all living together! And it's very, very wet and usually hot. The rainforest is teeming with life.

Malayan tapirs

We spend most of our time in trees and build big nests in the branches to sleep in.

Orangutans

When I'm a baby I'm stripy to help me hide from predators.

Like many rainforest animals, we are at risk of extinction (dying out) and need protection.

How much does it rain?

A lot! Most rainforests get at least two metres of rain a year. Water drips from all the leaves, high up and low down. The hot, wet air makes you feel sticky.

Sometimes i use a large leaf as an umbrella!

Is it all just trees?

No – there are lots of different kinds of plants packed into a rainforest, from soaring trees to tiny mosses. Some plants, such as epiphytes, even grow on others.

Epiphyte

Fire-tufted barbet

Hornbill

Most bird species in the rainforests aren't found anywhere else in the world.

Sumatran tiger

Do lots of animals live there?

Yes! Rainforests have the greatest variety of living things of any places on Earth, from tiny insects to bigger animals such as tigers and elephants.

Are there rivers in a rainforest?

Many rainforests have lots of rivers, fed by all the rain. The rivers of the Amazon rainforest contain a fifth of all the world's fresh water.

Sumatran elephant

Where are the rainforests?

Rainforests grow where there is plenty of rain, all year. Many lie in a region called the tropics where it's hot and sunny as well as wet.

Mountain gorillas

Elk like me are large deer that live in temperate rainforests in North America.

Elk

Temperate rainforests have huge evergreen trees. Some have bears, mountain lions and elk.

North America

Europe

South America

KEY
Cloud forest

Tropical rainforest

Temperate rainforest

Are there different types?

Yes. As well as hot **tropical rainforests**, there are **temperate rainforests** in cooler rainy areas and misty **cloud forests** in the mountains.

The cloud forests of Africa are our home. We live in family groups and eat plants and insects.

Asia

Oceania

Africa

We live in Madagascar.

Can a forest grow in the clouds?

Yes! Cloud forests grow on mountains where air carrying moisture cools. Tiny water droplets form, making clouds at the level of the treetops.

We like sunbathing in the morning to warm up after the cool night.

Ring-tailed lemurs

Do the same animals live in each one?

Not at all. Most rainforests have a lot of species (kinds of plant or animal) found nowhere else, such as the lemurs of Madagascar.

Did you know?

HISS!

The enormous **atlas moth** has a wing span of 30 centimetres. Its wing tips look like the head of a snake to ward off predators.

Piranhas are fierce fish of the Amazon that can make a barking sound and gnash their teeth.

WOOF!

The **hoatzin** bird of South America is also called the stink bird because its whole body smells like manure.

Bromeliad plants store their own water. Rain collects in the middle of the plant. A large bromeliad can hold up to 8 litres of water.

The Amazon's **anaconda** is the biggest snake in the world. It can be over 5 metres long and weigh almost 100 kilograms.

Green iguanas can run up to 34 kilometres per hour!

A **jaguar** can bite through the skull of a crocodile or the shell of a turtle. And it likes to swim, so nowhere is safe.

Leaf cutter ants are some of the strongest creatures on Earth.

They can carry leaves 50 times as heavy as themselves!

South American **emerald boas** are born red, yellow or orange and turn green when about a year old.

One **poison dart frog** has enough poison on its skin to kill 10 people.

What is it like in the rainforest?

It's hot and sticky, teeming with life and very green! At ground level, you can hardly see the sky as the millions of plants and trees block out most of the sunlight.

HOWL

SNARL

GROWL

HOOT

I need to sleep in the day – but it's so noisy!

Bushbaby

What can you hear?

There are strange noises coming from every corner with chattering and chirping, howls, hoots, growls and hisses. You can hear the patter of rain, the rustling of leaves and animals' footsteps.

I feed on fruit and sugary tree sap and grow up to 11 centimetres long!

Goliath beetle

Chimpanzee

We chimps use the rainforest's hanging vines to swing from tree to tree.

How does the forest pack in so many plants?

Many plants grow on top of others. Vines called lianas grow up and around tall trees and epiphytes grow on branches and in cracks.

Grey parrot

The air is hot and still all the time. Wind doesn't reach the ground.

HISS

African bush viper

Is it crowded?

Plants block every step of the way. Although trees don't have branches low down, fallen branches, dead leaves, bushes, ferns, vines and tree roots cover most of the ground.

Is it all a big tangle?

No. Rainforests have four layers. At the top is the overstorey, followed by the canopy, full of trees and vines. The understorey grows around the giant tree trunks, and the forest floor is where the plants are rooted.

The overstorey is windy, with more direct sunlight and rain than lower down.

The canopy is a continuous blanket of tall trees all fighting for sunlight.

Harpy eagle

I perch at the tops of trees looking for animals to eat.

Scarlet macaw

I eat seeds and fruit in the treetops.

Sloth

I only come down to the forest floor once every week or two to poo.

Howler monkey

I make one of the loudest noises of any animal. You can hear me from miles away!

How many?

11.9 Annual rainfall in metres in the wettest rainforest on Earth, in India. That's 12 times as deep as the shallow end of a swimming pool.

80 Wingbeats per second of the bee hummingbird — the smallest bird in the world.

89.5 Height in metres of the largest tropical tree in the world, a Yellow Meranti in the Malaysian rainforest.

The number of extra plants that can live on a single rainforest tree, making up a third of the tree's weight is **2000**

Hey, what's it like up there?

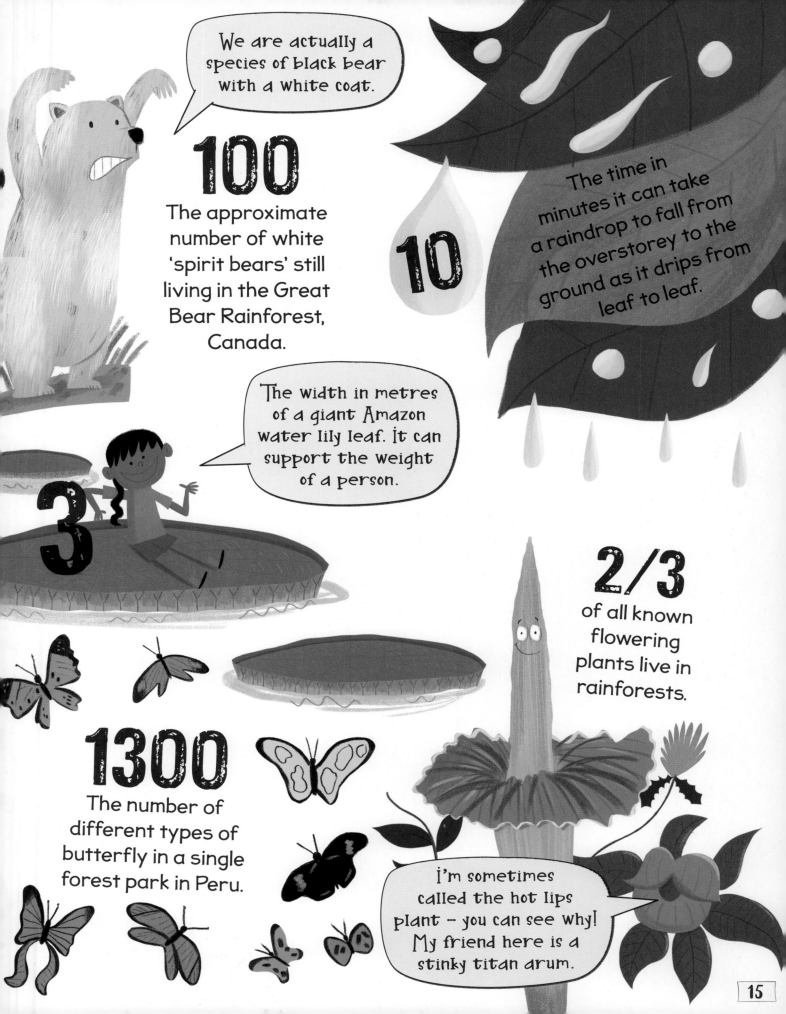

We are actually a species of black bear with a white coat.

100
The approximate number of white 'spirit bears' still living in the Great Bear Rainforest, Canada.

10
The time in minutes it can take a raindrop to fall from the overstorey to the ground as it drips from leaf to leaf.

The width in metres of a giant Amazon water lily leaf. It can support the weight of a person.

3

2/3
of all known flowering plants live in rainforests.

1300
The number of different types of butterfly in a single forest park in Peru.

I'm sometimes called the hot lips plant – you can see why! My friend here is a stinky titan arum.

What do the trees eat for dinner?

Trees make their own food by using the energy from sunlight, chemicals in the air, and water. This is called photosynthesis. Tree roots also take chemicals from the soil to help them grow big and strong.

We birds eat insects, grubs, seeds, fruit and nectar.

Sri Lankan blue magpie

Sri Lankan grey hornbill

Does anything eat the giant trees?

Nothing eats a whole tree! But everything from tiny insects to large animals like monkeys and elephants eat leaves, fruit, seeds and nectar. Many eat tiny plants, too.

Loten's sunbird

My long beak fits right into flowers to reach sticky nectar.

Purple-faced leaf monkey

Hey, watch out!

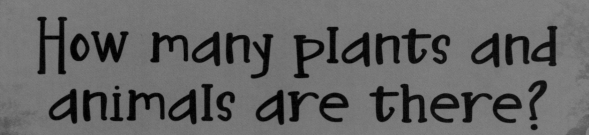

How many plants and animals are there?

A lot! Rainforests have the biggest range of living things on Earth. Although they cover just 6 percent of the land, more than 50 percent of all plant and animal species live here.

Scientists first saw me in 2010...

Fire-tailed titi monkey

...and they first heard me singing my sweet song in 2009.

Chico's tyrannulet

Have we found everything yet?

Not by a long way. Scientists have studied only a small portion of rainforest species. After just one expedition to the Amazon in 2014–15, a total of 381 new species were named.

Are there any dragons?

Yes! Boyd's forest dragons live in Australia's rainforest. They aren't real dragons but are a type of lizard that lives in trees and feasts on rainforest insects.

Boyd's forest dragon

I live in the Daintree and have spines on my legs that can puncture skin!

Spiny leaf insect

Rosy periwinkle

Which is the oldest rainforest?

The Daintree rainforest in Australia is over 100 million years old. It has 3000 species of plant and 12,000 species of insect.

Which plants are the most powerful?

Many rainforest plants help make medicines that fight disease. I'm from Madagascar and contain chemicals that are used in drugs to treat cancer.

What's the weirdest thing in the rainforest?

Maybe plants that eat animals! Carnivorous plants found in some cloud forests can trap small animals and dissolve them for their dinner!

Sundew plant

Eek! I'm caught in the sundew's sticky blobs and need to escape before I become lunch.

Goliath bird-eating spider

Yum!

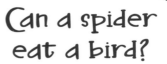

Can a spider eat a bird?

Yes, if it's a South American Goliath bird-eating spider. It's the world's heaviest spider at 170 grams and is as big as a dinner plate! It usually eats insects, small mammals (like mice) and lizards.

When is a tree stump not a tree stump?

When it's a potoo bird in the Amazon! These insect-eaters hunt at night and perch camouflaged on tree stumps during the day.

Pretend I'm not here.

Potoo

Hey, get off! This is my neck of the woods!

Do strawberries fight each other?

No, but tiny strawberry poison-dart frogs do! Like many similar frogs, they wrestle each other for the best nest sites and territories.

Flies love this awful smell because they like to lay their eggs in rotting meat.

Which flower smells of rotting meat?

The giant rafflesia flower in Indonesia! It's one metre wide, and its nasty pong attracts flies that pollinate the flower.

Would you rather?

Swing from vines with the **monkeys**...

...or climb a tall tree with a **spectacled bear**?

Be a super-strong **titan beetle** that can snap pencils with its jaws...

Eat a fresh tropical **pineapple** or make your own chocolate from hand-picked **cocoa beans**?

...or a pretty **firefly beetle** with a glow-in-the-dark tummy?

Be a beautiful **bird-of-paradise** with cool dance moves that attract a mate...

...or a speedy **cassowary** that can run through the rainforest at 50 kilometres an hour?

When trekking through the rainforest, would you rather come across a **blood-sucking leech** or a **giant hairy spider**?

Get up close to a **jaguar** in the Amazon or a **gorilla** in the Congo?

Visit a hot and steamy **tropical rainforest**...

...or a cool and rainy **cloud forest**?

Do people live in the rainforest?

Yes. Some tribes (groups of people) have lived in rainforests for thousands of years and still do. Some live in much the same way as their ancestors.

We catch fish from the river and find food in the forest.

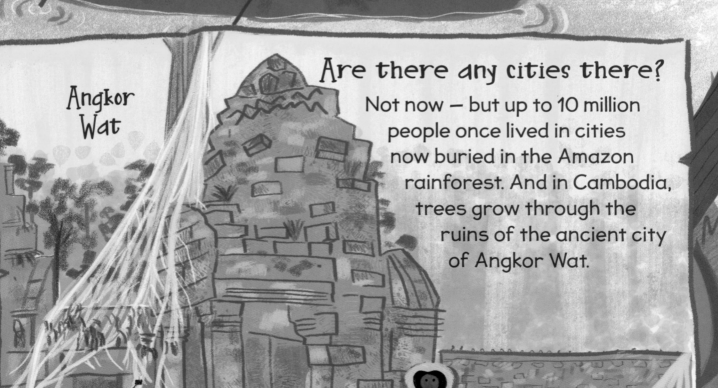

Angkor Wat

Are there any cities there?

Not now — but up to 10 million people once lived in cities now buried in the Amazon rainforest. And in Cambodia, trees grow through the ruins of the ancient city of Angkor Wat.

Sloth

Who works in the rainforest?

Scientists track and investigate the plants and animals that live there. Also, some people are farmers, growing and collecting cocoa, coffee, rubber and other rainforest crops.

> I'm helping us learn more about the different species in the rainforest.

Is it dangerous?

It can be. There are some large animals that could attack you, like jaguars or crocodiles. There are lots of poisonous animals that could sting or bite you, including snakes, spiders and insects. And it's very easy to get lost!

Amazon tree boa

> Tiny mosquitoes carry deadly diseases and cause more deaths than any other animal in the world.

Mosquito

What happens at night?

Lots of things – all the nocturnal animals come out. These creatures hunt or feed in the rainforest by night to keep safe from predators or to stay out of the daytime heat.

Madagascar long-eared owl

I hunt at night to grab small animals that are out looking for their own food.

Aye-aye

I tap tree bark and listen for grubs inside, then I wiggle them out with my freaky long finger.

Flying fox

I'm a type of bat. I come out after dark to feast on fruit.

I only live for five days so have to find a mate quickly so we can lay eggs.

Mouse lemur

There are lots of different types of lemurs in Madagascar and some of us come out at night.

Comet moth

Most of us frogs are nocturnal. You can hear us croaking at night-time.

Tree frog

When frightened, I blow myself up full of air, looking even more like a tomato!

Tomato frog

Tenrec

I'm a large cat-like mammal and I'll eat almost anything. I hunt by day or night.

Fossa

I'm spiky, like a hedgehog, and hunt for grubs and insects on the forest floor.

Tufted-tail rat

It's dangerous on the forest floor, even at night. I eat plants, but lots of animals want to eat me!

Are rainforests in danger?

Yes, and we need to look after them. Rainforests around the world are threatened by people.

There used to be lots more rainforest. It's being cut down all the time, making animals homeless.

Clearing the rainforest is called deforestation and it affects our climate.

Large areas are also burned down to clear land for crops or beef cattle.

Around one-sixth of the Amazon rainforest has been destroyed.

Destroyed rainforest

Amazon rainforest

South America

Why do we need rainforests?

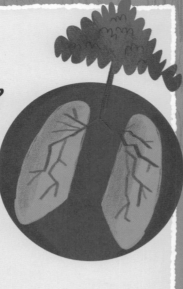

Life on Earth needs the right balance of oxygen and carbon dioxide in the atmosphere.

The plants and trees of the rainforest take carbon dioxide in and put oxygen back into the air, which all animals need.

How can we save the rainforests?

Everyone can make a difference. You can avoid beef from areas where rainforest has been cleared...

...and can ask your government to protect these areas and the people and wildlife that live there.

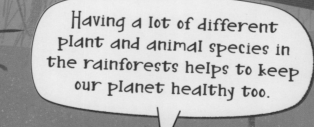

Having a lot of different plant and animal species in the rainforests helps to keep our planet healthy too.

A compendium of questions

Which animal smells like hot popcorn?

I do! I'm a binturong, from Southeast Asia. I have a gland under my tail that makes a popcorn smell.

Why are some sloths green?

Because tiny plants called algae grow in our fur!

Does an anteater only eat ants?

It eats ants or termites with its super-long tongue. A giant anteater can eat up to 35,000 in a single day!

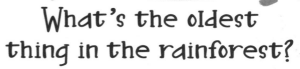

Can we eat rainforest plants?

Yes, some of them. Lots of fruit and nuts first came from the rainforest, including tomatoes, pineapples, Brazil nuts and potatoes.

What's the oldest thing in the rainforest?

Some trees in the temperate rainforest of Tasmania are 2000 years old.